MW01280294

6489

Alternative Energy

by Cherese Cartlidge

ERICKSON PRESS
Yankton, South Dakota

ERICKSON PRESS

For more information, contact
Erickson Press
329 Broadway
PO Box 33
Yankton, SD 57078

Or you can visit our Internet site at www.ericksonpress.com

LIBRARY OF CONGRESS CATALOGING-IN-PUBLICATION DATA

Cartlidge, Cherese.
  Alternative energy / by Cherese Cartlidge.
    p. cm. — (Ripped from the headlines)
  Includes bibliographical references and index.
Summary: This high-interest book for low-reading-level students considers the drawbacks of burning fossil fuels and the growing need to use renewable, nonpolluting sources of energy. The development and use of these sources are discussed, including geothermal, solar, and nuclear energy; power obtained from wind, water, and hydrogen; and the growing use of biofuel.
  ISBN: 978-1-60217-022-3 (hardcover : alk. paper)
  1. Renewable energy sources—Juvenile literature. I. Title.
  TJ808.2.C36 2008
  333.79'4—dc22
                                                          2007043699

Printed in the United States of America

Contents

Alternative Energy at Work

A concrete tower stands in Seville, Spain. It is forty stories tall. Bright rays of light shine all around it. The light comes from 600 mirrors in the tower. The mirrors help turn sunlight into electricity. Six hundred thousand people live in Seville. The tower makes enough power for the entire city.

This pale yellow tower is much taller than the other buildings nearby. The beams of light that shine from it make the air around it seem to glow. One man who visited the tower said it "looked like it was being hosed with giant sprays of water or was somehow being squirted with jets of pale gas. . . . [Actually] the rays of sunlight reflected by a field of 600 huge mirrors are so intense they illuminate the water vapour and dust hanging in the air."[1]

The tower in Seville shows one use of alternative energy. *Alternative* means something that is different from what is usual. Until the Industrial Revolution in the mid-1700s, humans relied mostly on wood for their energy. Then they started burning coal to make power for factories. In the mid-1800s petroleum began to be used in factories and homes when the United States started refining oil. Coal and petroleum, along with natural gas, are forms of fossil fuels. These come from plants and animals that lived millions of years ago.

Today 90 percent of energy used in the world comes from fossil fuels. But burning fossil fuels causes many problems. The main problem with fossil fuels is that they cannot be renewed. They will run out and cannot be replaced. Fossil fuels also pollute the air when they are burned. They cause

Pump jacks pull oil out of the ground.

smog that makes it hard for people to breathe. They also give off carbon dioxide. This traps heat around the earth. That adds to the problem of global warming.

Nations around the world want to find good ways to reduce the use of fossil fuels. They want types of power that do not pollute. These are better for the planet. And they are better for people's health. Nations also want to use power that can be replaced. Some places plan to use more of this type of power. By 2010 the European Union plans to get 22 percent of its power from alternative energy.

There are many ways of making power. Humans can make power from the sun, wind, water, and many other sources. These forms of power do not pollute. And they can be replaced. But each of these forms of power also has its own set of problems. That is why people must keep working to improve all forms of alternative energy.

Chapter 1

Solar Energy

The sun shines a lot in Sarnia. But it is not a very warm place. Sarnia is in Ontario, Canada. Winds from the Arctic blow through Sarnia. In winter it can get as cold as -15°F (-26°C). And the cold weather can last up to eight months. Summers are warmer. But they do not last long. And they are not all that warm. A summer day is usually 68°F (20°C). Yet Sarnia is still an ideal place for solar power. It will soon have the largest solar power station in North America.

A solar power station uses solar panels to turn sunlight into electricity. The station near Sarnia will cover about 902 acres (365ha) of land. That is as much as 682 football fields. It will have about 1 million solar panels. The solar panels will stretch as high as 23 feet (7m). From the air these panels will look like rows of blue theater seats in a field.

On sunny days the station will make enough power for about 6,000 to 8,000 homes. That is about 25 percent of the homes in Sarnia. On cloudy days the station will still be able to make power.

Solar panels reflect light toward a central tower in Seville, Spain.

But it will make much less power than on sunny days. When it is cloudy, people will have to get more power from other sources.

Peter Carrie is the vice president of the company that is building the Sarnia power station. He says, "This is certainly the most exciting thing I've ever worked on."[2] Carrie adds, "Solar electricity is just about everything we could want in an energy source. . . . It's clean, you can tap into it wherever and whenever the sun shines. It's quiet, sustainable and Earth-friendly."[3]

Sandra is a girl who lives in Canada. She is excited about the new plant that will be built near Sarnia. Sandra says, "I think that's awesome! We're finally doing something about reducing greenhouse gases! I wish that more places used solar power so that our planet wouldn't be polluted."[4]

Solar Power Around the World

Sarnia's solar power station shows how the sun can be used to make electricity. This can be done even in a cold northern town like Sarnia. The sunlight is not as hot or bright in Sarnia as it is in other

2007 Solar Decathlon

In October 2007 twenty solar homes took a trip. They went to the National Mall. It is in Washington, D.C. The solar homes were part of the third Solar Decathlon. This is a contest run by the Department of Energy (DOE). The DOE is trying to find ways to make solar power cost less money. The homes in this contest must get all their power from the sun.

Twenty teams entered the contest. The teams came from colleges and universities in the United States, Puerto Rico, Spain, Germany, and Canada. The teams had to design and build their own solar homes. Then they had to move them to the National Mall. They had to rebuild them in the "solar village." The teams were judged in ten areas. These areas included design, comfort, and power creation. The German team won first place. After the decathlon, the house returned to the university in Germany and served as a solar power plant.

places. Yet the sun still shines enough to make the power for thousands of homes.

Many other solar power stations exist around the world. They can be found in Algeria, Australia, Canada, France, Germany, Japan, Portugal, Spain, and the United States. Other countries plan to build solar power stations soon. These include Brazil, China, and Israel. Right now Germany makes more solar power than any other country. It makes about half of all the solar power made in the world.

One reason so many countries use solar power is because it is safe. It does not pollute. Solar power can also be renewed. That means the sun creates more light all the time. In fact, the sun makes more light than the earth can use. According to one solar

A project in Washington State explores new ways of getting solar power.

Energy Use in the United States

All Energy Sources

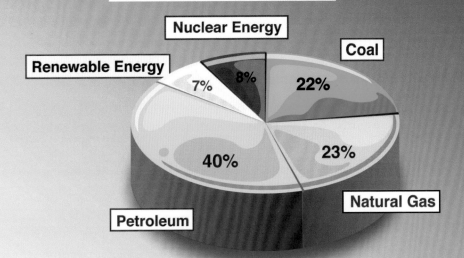

Nuclear Energy

Coal

Renewable Energy

7%

8%

22%

23%

40%

Natural Gas

Petroleum

Renewable Energy Sources

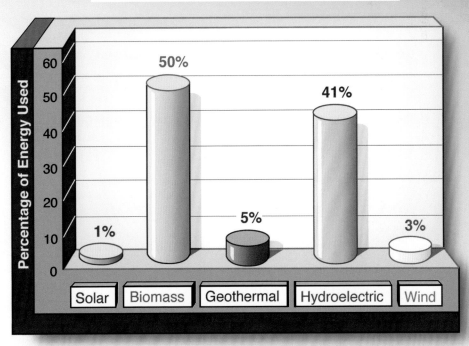

Percentage of Energy Used

50%

41%

5%

1%

3%

Solar | Biomass | Geothermal | Hydroelectric | Wind

Source: www.eia.doe.gov.

power Web site, "Every hour, the sun radiates more energy onto the earth than the entire human population uses in one whole year."[5]

Right now solar power is not used as much as other forms of power. This is because solar power stations cost a lot of money to build. The one near Sarnia will cost about $300 million to build. This makes solar power cost more than power made from other means. In the United States, solar electricity costs about 25 to 50 cents per kilowatt-hour. That is about five times as much as electricity from fossil fuels.

Another issue is the amount of land needed for solar power stations. The U.S. government estimates that it would take 11,848 square miles (30,685 sq. km) to make enough solar energy to meet half of the nation's power. At that rate, for the United States to rely on solar power for 100 percent of its energy, it would require roughly half the land area of Oregon. The fact that solar stations take up so much land makes some people question whether solar energy is a good solution. One concerned blogger states: "You'd only be able to build in certain areas, mostly the flat or gently sloping hills. Given these requirements, a solar powered North America would probably require the entire usable land of Nevada and Utah."[6]

Solar Panels

But solar power stations are not the only way to get power from the sun. A home or building with solar panels can do that, too. Solar power can heat water

Baboon-Proof Solar Power

The baboons in Tanzania, Africa had a surprise for Jeff Lahl. He works for a group that brings solar power to remote places. He put up solar panels at the Jane Goodall Institute in 2005. He said the hardest part about this job was the baboons. Lahl had to take extra care "so that little nimble fingers could not grasp exposed wire to hang or swing from."

He says the baboons "love to run and thunder across the metal roofs of the research center and like to jump, sit, lie, and sleep on the few existing solar modules on the roof at the research center. They must like the smooth surface. They usually only stay on the modules for a few minutes, so there's not [a] big loss of power. The benefit is that their fur keeps the modules clean and dusted."

Baboons in Tanzania "dusted" their new solar panels.

Quoted in Solar Electric Light Fund, "Solar Energy: Clean, Reliable, Sustainable—and Baboon-Proof." www.self.org/tanzania2.asp.

to be used for washing, bathing, and cooking. In the United States solar power is mainly used to heat swimming pools. In China around 30 million homes have solar water heaters. Homes and buildings are also built to make the best use of sunlight for heat and light. Getting power from the sun in these ways does not cost a lot of money.

Solar power is used in another important way. It is used to bring electricity to rural areas. This can be seen in a small village in South Africa. The village is called Maphaphethe. Sixteen thousand people live there. Maphaphethe is not connected to the power grid. That means it does not get power from an electric company. People in this village do not know if they will ever get electric or telephone services like big cities.

The government wanted to change that. It started a program in 1996 to bring solar power to Maphaphethe. It did this with help from a nonprofit group. They put solar panels on the roofs of homes. For the first time people there have electric lights in their homes. They can also watch television. Solar power has changed their lives.

Each solar home system includes one solar panel on the roof. It also includes a battery, wiring, light fixtures, and switches. Each system costs $600. Families buy them on credit. They pay a small amount each month.

The solar systems do not make a lot of power. There is only enough for three fluorescent lightbulbs. And the lights can only be on for five hours a day. The televisions have to be black and white.

Solar panels are installed on the roof of a Minnesota junior high school.

But the homes have electricity. That is something the people of Maphaphethe never had before.

The program also brought solar power to the high school. Now the school has computers. For the first time students can surf the Internet. Samantha Dlomo goes to the high school. She explains how her life has changed:

> Solar energy has not only changed my school life, it has brightened up my future as well. I am sixteen years old and have lived in the rural area for the past fourteen years. In all these past years I used a candle stick to study and do my homework. . . . Solar energy has brightened my future and it is destined to brighten the future of millions of others.[7]

So far there are 54 solar homes in Maphaphethe. The program is a pilot project. That means it is a test. The government wants to see how well the solar homes work. They hope to bring solar homes to more people. There are 3.7 million families in South Africa who have no power. The government hopes to have 2.5 million solar homes by 2015. Other countries are trying projects like the one in Maphaphethe. They also hope to bring solar power to people who do not have power.

The Promise of Solar Power

Solar power is not used as much as it could be. But many people are trying to change that. Experts are trying to find ways to lower the cost of getting power from the sun. One way they are doing this is with cheaper materials.

Solar panels are made up of cells. These cells are made of silicon. Silicon is an element found in sand. Cells made from silicon cost a lot. Several companies are making a new kind of solar cell. It does not cost much money.

This new type of cell is made from tiny molecules of carbon in a tube shape. These carbon molecules are called nanotubes. Experts say nanotubes are 50,000 times smaller than a human hair. And they are very good at conducting electricity.

The new cells can be painted or printed onto flexible plastic sheets. The sheets can then be put onto walls or rooftops to make solar power. Someday people might be able to print their own flexible solar panels at home. They could print them on inkjet printers. The cells could also be painted right onto items. They could be painted on calculators, cell phones, and iPods. Someday they may even be put on cars. One expert says, "Imagine some day driving in your hybrid car with a solar panel painted on the roof, which is producing electricity to drive the engine. The opportunities are endless. . . . Someday, I hope to see this process become an inexpensive energy alternative for households around the world."[8] Experts think these new cells could make five times more solar power than the ones being used now.

A Missouri farmer shows off his solar-powered tractor.

Solar Power in Outer Space

Solar power is used for many things on Earth. It is also used for lots of things in outer space. In 2004 two robots were sent to explore Mars. They are named Spirit and Opportunity. Each robot has many solar panels. One NASA Web site says, "They look almost like 'wings,' but their purpose is to provide energy, not fly." Satellites in space use solar panels, too. Some of them relay television signals back to Earth.

Mars Exploration Rover Mission: The Mission, "Spacecraft: Surface Operations: Rover: The Rover's Energy." http://mars.jpl.nasa.gov/mer/mission/spacecraft_rover_energy.html.

Other experts have made another new type of solar cell. It also costs less than silicon cells. These cells are made with a mixture of white metal-oxide powder and red dye. The red and white colors mix and make the cells look pink. These new pink cells are not as good at making solar power as silicon cells. But they cost only one-fourth as much to make. And experts hope that soon the pink solar cells will make power as well as silicon cells do.

The promise of solar power is great. The sun is a never-ending source of heat and light. Every day people find new ways to use the power of the sun. Soon making power from the sun may cost much less than it does now. Then solar power might take the place of power from other sources.

Chapter 2

Nuclear Energy and Hydrogen

Agroup of buildings sits at the bottom of a grassy hill. In the middle of the buildings are two big domes. Beyond the buildings a 230-foot (70m) granite cliff drops down to the sea. This is the Flamanville nuclear power plant. It is on the northern coast of France. The two domes hold the nuclear reactors. Soon there will be a third reactor. It will be called the Flamanville 3. The Flamanville 3 will be France's 59th nuclear reactor. It will cost $4.4 billion dollars (3.3 billion euros) to build. The new reactor will be finished in 2012. It will make enough electricity for 1.5 million people.

The element uranium is used for nuclear power. Nuclear power is clean. It does not pollute the air. Countries all around the world use nuclear power. France is the world leader in nuclear power. It gets more than 80 percent of its power from nuclear plants. One French nuclear physicist says, "We have a joke in France, 'No coal, no oil, no gas, no choice.' But I don't like that joke. I think we have a very good choice—nuclear." [9]

Nuclear power plants may be a way to get clean electricity.

A few countries, such as Germany and Denmark, plan to stop using nuclear power. They are doing this because of safety concerns. But other countries want to build more nuclear plants. They think nuclear power is a safe way to get clean electricity.

Nuclear Power

Nuclear power works by splitting uranium atoms. This takes place in a reactor. There is water in the reactor. The atoms release heat when they are split. This heats up the water and makes steam. The steam is used to power electric generators.

Splitting uranium atoms to make nuclear power also creates radioactive material. This material gives off rays that are harmful or poisonous to people. That means nuclear power can be very dangerous.

Nuclear power was first used in the 1940s. Its use soon increased around the world. But that changed in the late 1970s. There was an accident at the Three Mile Island nuclear power plant in the United States in 1979. Some radioactive gas leaked into the air. It was only a small amount of gas. But it caused an increase in the amount of radiation

A Warning for the Future

Nuclear waste stays radioactive for thousands of years. One way to get rid of nuclear waste is to bury it. It must be put in safe containers deep below the ground. And it must stay buried for thousands of years.

Nuclear waste burial sites need some sort of permanent signs to warn future generations it is dangerous to dig or drill there. But people in the future may no longer speak any of the languages we speak today. They may no longer recognize any of the symbols we use today for danger. So one man came up with an idea to warn people of the future to stay away from these sites. His idea was to place 50-foot-tall (15m) concrete spires all around the site. The spires would have concrete spikes coming out of them. His design is called the Landscape of Thorns. These "thorns" would give people the idea that it was not safe to be in the area.

R.C. Baker, "Deep Time, Short Sight: Bracing for Yucca Mountain's Nuclear Forever," *Village Voice*, May 25, 2002. www.villagevoice.com/news/0222, baker,35183,1.html.

people in the area were exposed to. Even though no one was seriously injured, many people began to have doubts about nuclear power.

In 1986 something else happened to make people afraid of nuclear power. There was a big explosion at the Chernobyl plant in the Soviet Union. It was the worst nuclear accident in history. The explosion sent out a radioactive cloud. This poisoned the air and the soil in the area. Two hundred thousand people had to move away. After this accident, some nations stopped building new plants. In the United States no new reactors have been ordered since 1978.

Now countries are again building reactors. These countries include France, Japan, and China. Other countries are talking about building new reactors as well. People are starting to think of nuclear ener-

One unit of an Alabama nuclear power plant was readied for service after a $1.8 billion makeover.

gy as a good way to get power without polluting the air. France uses nuclear power a lot. It has the cleanest air in the industrialized world. It also has the lowest electric bills in Europe.

Anne Lauvergeon is an engineer. In France she is known as "Atomic Anne." Lauvergeon has a good reason why nuclear power is a good choice. "You have hydro, you have nuclear, you have wind and you have solar. But wind and solar are you know, temporary sources of energy. It works when you have wind, it works when you have sun. No sun, no wind, no energy. You don't want to watch TV only when you have wind." [10]

Building a Better Reactor

Another country that is building new nuclear plants is China. It is making a new type of reactor. This reactor has 27,000 balls of uranium in it. The balls are wrapped in layers of strong materials that resist melting. The uranium is safe inside these balls. That is because the balls have a higher melting point than the reactor could ever reach. If something goes wrong the reactor will just shut down. This type of reactor is called a pebblebed reactor.

Edwin deSteiguer Snead wants to build a nuclear power plant in Texas. He went to China in early 2006. There he toured a model of the pebblebed reactor. After the tour Snead said, "So let me see if I can describe it in Texas English. There's no way it can explode or melt?" The Chinese experts agreed with him. Snead was impressed. He said, "I think the Americans will be buying nuclear plants from China within five years."[11]

Hydrogen Fuel Cells

In Utah hundreds of excited people were about to see hydrogen at work. They were at the 2007 Speed Week. This event is held every year at the Bonneville Salt Flats. The people shielded their eyes from the sun. Suddenly a bright green and silver car flew past them. It was going over 207 miles per hour (333km/h). The big number 999 painted in white on its sides was just a blur. This was the Ford Fusion Hydrogen 999. It had just set a world speed record for a fuel-cell car. The car did not run on gasoline. It was powered by a hydrogen fuel cell.

The Fusion 999 is a one-of-a-kind car. No other hydrogen fuel-cell car in the world can go as fast as it can. Matt Zuehlk is the lead engineer on the project. He says, "What we've accomplished is nothing short of an industry first. No other automaker in the world has come close."[12] Still, many countries around the world are looking at fuel cells. They want to find ways to make fuel cells more affordable. If they can, more cars can be built with fuel cells in them. And more people can drive cars that do not pollute.

Hydrogen is used in many ways to make power. One is liquid rocket fuel. Another is fuel cells. They are kind of like batteries. Fuel cells can generate electricity. President George W. Bush wants American automakers to use fuel cells in cars. At a speech on Earth Day in 2006 he said, "I strongly believe hydrogen is the fuel of the future." [13]

One automaker gives a good reason to drive fuel-cell cars. It asks, "Have you ever had to roll up your windows to keep from choking on the exhaust from an older car in front of you?" [14] With cars that use fuel cells, this is not a problem. Their only waste product is clean water. In fact, the wastewater from a fuel cell is clean enough to drink.

Many carmakers are working on hydrogen fuel-cell vehicles. Several model cars and buses are being tested. One example is the Honda FCX. Honda plans to start selling the car to the public by 2018.

Honda shows off its FCX, a planned hydrogen fuel-cell car.

Earth-Friendly Fuel-Cell Cars

The Honda FCX uses hydrogen for its power. So it does not release carbon dioxide into the air like regular cars. This car helps the earth in another way. The seats of old cars are burned when they are taken to a junkyard. The seats of the Honda FCX are made from a special type of fabric. Honda calls it "bio-fabric." This fabric is long-lasting. And it is made from specially grown plants. These plants absorb lots of carbon dioxide when they are growing. That helps make up for the carbon dioxide they release when they are burned.

Tara Weingarten took a test model of the FCX for a drive. She describes what it was like to drive one of these super-quiet cars:

> I turned the key and heard a whir as air mixed with hydrogen. I stepped on the gas—make that *hydrogen*-gas pedal—and launched forward with a powerful pull. All was silent. That's because the FCX's hydrogen is used to create power for an electric motor. The car sounds like a golf cart, albeit one with a few kitchen-blender-sounding whirs from the mixing of gases, and maybe a slight whine, like that of a very quiet aircraft engine. And then, wow. The FCX accelerates at freeway on-ramp speed, it brakes equally well and the steering is sharp.

Hydrogen Fuel Cell

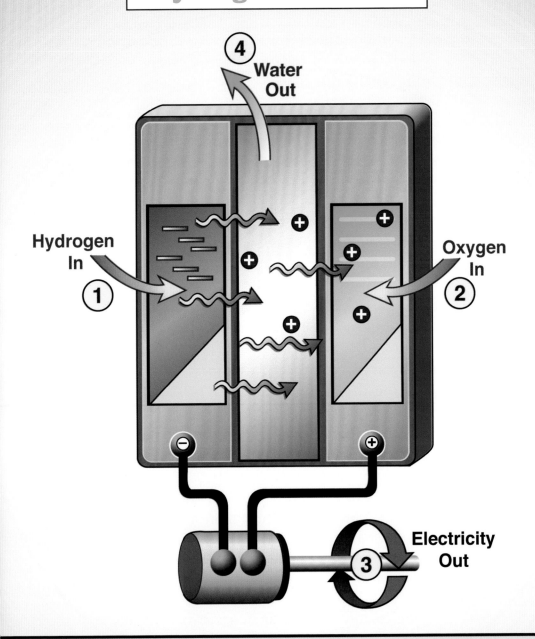

Hydrogen fuel cells work by changing hydrogen **(1)** and oxygen **(2)** into water. By doing this, the fuel cell produces electricity **(3)**. The only waste product is clear water **(4)**. Fuel cells do not cause pollution.

Source: www.eia.doe.gov.

I hardly noticed it was powered different-ly from any of today's vehicles, except for its remarkable silence. [15]

Fuel cells work by changing hydrogen and oxygen into water. Doing this makes electricity. Fuel cells do not pollute. And hydrogen is easy to replace. In fact, it is the most common element there is.

One reason fuel cells are not used more is the expense. Many of the parts used to build them cost a lot of money. Fuel cells use platinum to help change the hydrogen and oxygen into water. Platinum is a precious metal. It is very costly. Experts are trying to make fuel cells cost less. They are testing fuel cells that use less platinum. They are also testing fuel cells that use nonprecious metals. These cost less than platinum.

Using the elements to make power can be a clean, safe, alternative way of getting energy. Scientists around the world are working on ways to make nuclear power plants safer and safer. Others are studying ways to make hydrogen power more of a reality. In the future, it is likely that both ways of making power will become more and more common throughout the world.

Chapter 3

Energy from Wind and Water

P rince Willem-Alexander of the Netherlands stood by the sea. It was a crisp day in April 2007. Fourteen children gathered around the prince. They were at a special ceremony. It was for the opening of the country's first offshore wind farm. The wind farm is in the North Sea. The prince and the children blew on plastic spinning fans in their hands. The spinning fans were symbols for the 36 windmills of the Egmond aan Zee Offshore Wind Farm.

The wind farm looks like a "metallic forest"[16] standing up in the shallow water. It makes enough power to light 100,000 homes. It is called "the Netherlands' cleanest power plant."[17] That is because wind farms do not pollute. This is the country's first offshore wind farm. It plans to build 65 wind farms in the North Sea.

Wind Power

Wind is a clean and safe source of power. One writer says, "For environmentalists, the windmill

Offshore windmills in the North Sea capture the power of the wind.

is a perfect alternative. The wind never runs out, and leaves no waste products behind."[18]

Europe is a world leader in using wind power. Denmark gets 20 percent of its power from wind. Germany and Spain get about 10 percent of their power from wind. Denmark plans to get even more power from wind in the future. Its goal is 50 percent by 2025. Germany also plans to use more wind power. It plans to get 20 percent of its power from wind by 2020. Sweden, Norway, and Finland are planning to use more wind power, too.

Large wind farms are built in places that get the most wind. But this leads to a problem. One writer explains, "Windy spots are often located far away from big urban centers that use the most power."[19] One reason for this is that big cities are not usually built on the sides of steep, windy canyons and so forth. This makes it cost more to get the power to cities. Power lines must be put in to carry the power to cities. That costs a lot of money.

Windmills come in different shapes and sizes.

Another issue is the amount of land required for large wind farms. One example is the Horse Hollow Wind Energy Center in Texas. It is the world's largest onshore wind farm. It has 421 wind turbines. The wind farm makes enough power for

It Depends on the Wind

One thing companies must consider when planning a wind farm is where to build it. The location depends on factors such as how fast the wind blows in different areas. The Energy Information Administration Web site explains that

wind speed varies throughout the country. It also varies from season to season. In Tehachapi, California, the wind blows more from April through October than it does in the winter. This is because of the extreme heating of the Mojave Desert during the summer months. The hot air over the desert rises, and the cooler, denser air above the Pacific Ocean rushes through the Tehachapi mountain pass to take its place. In a state like Montana, on the other hand, the wind blows more during the winter. Fortunately, these seasonal variations are a good match for the electricity demands of the regions. In California, people use more electricity during the summer for air conditioners. In Montana, people use more electricity during the winter months for heating.

Energy Kid's Page, "Wind Energy—Energy from Moving Air." www.eia.doe.gov/kids/energyfacts/sources/renewable/wind.html.

230,000 homes per year. But the wind farm takes up about 73 square miles (189 sq. km) of land. At that rate, in order to power a city the size of Columbus, Ohio, it would take about as much land area as a slightly smaller city, about the size of Lincoln, Nebraska, covered with wind turbines.

Thrifty Power

Wind power can be used cheaply in places. One example of this is at the Jiminy Peak Mountain Resort. It is in Hancock, Massachusetts. In August 2007 the ski resort set a record. It began making its own power from a single windmill. It is the first private business in North America to do that.

The windmill is named the Zephyr. It will make about one-third of the ski resort's power. It will lower the resort's power costs by 50 percent a year. The resort's Web site says the Zephyr is part of its "efforts to preserve the Earth for future generations." [20]

Experts are working on ways to make power from wind farms cost less so it can be used more. One way is by changing the design of windmills. A windmill that is used to make power is called a turbine. Turbines usually have three blades. They look like the propeller on an airplane. Making the blades longer helps each turbine create more power. This helps keep the cost down. One writer explains that the lower costs are "partly due to the advent of wind turbines with giant blades that sweep a circle as [far across] . . . as a football field." [21] But the giant blades can cause another problem. Birds can be killed by the spinning blades of the windmills. These turbines can be 400 feet (122m) tall or more. The blades spin as fast as 180 miles per hour (290km/h) at the tip. Wind farms can also disrupt the migration paths of birds that fly around them.

Building big wind farms disturbs land and wildlife. And wind turbines are noisy. People who live nearby complain they can hear the blades flicking in the wind. Wind farms can also cause poor television reception.

Part of the solution to these problems is building wind farms far away from homes. That is why countries like the Netherlands are building wind farms in the sea. But this adds to the cost because the power has to be moved a long distance.

The main reason wind power is not used more is that wind is variable. It does not blow at a steady rate all the time. So wind power is not reliable enough to be counted on as a major source of power.

Hydropower

The Three Gorges Dam in China is the largest hydroelectric river dam in the world. It is on the Yangtze River. The Yangtze is the third-longest river in the world. The Three Gorges Dam is 1.5 miles (2.3km) long. It is 607 feet (185m) tall. It is made of 989 million cubic feet (28 million cu. m) of concrete. It took 463,000 tons (470,408t) of steel to build the Three Gorges Dam. The reservoir, or water the dam holds back, is nearly 400 miles (654km) long. One reporter says, "It is being called

China's huge Three Gorges Dam will supply power to fifteen provinces.

the largest construction project in China since the Great Wall." [22]

The dam will be finished in 2009. Each year 79 trillion gallons (300 trillion L) of water will flow through the dam. The power plant will send power to fifteen provinces in China. The plant is expected to make as much power as eighteen nuclear power plants.

Turbines also use the movement of water to make power. This is called hydropower. Hydropower is used around the world. It makes about 20 percent of all power used in the world.

In some countries hydropower is the main power source. Norway gets nearly all its power from hydropower. The country has lots of fjords and

This hydroelectric plant makes power for thousands of Southern California households.

waterfalls. So the people there have always relied on hydropower. The Democratic Republic of the Congo (DRC) gets about 99 percent of its power from hydropower. The DRC has many rivers, including the powerful Congo River. The main power plant in the DRC is at Inga Falls on the Congo. Brazil gets 95 percent of its power from hydropower. It relies on the mighty Amazon River for its hydropower.

One reason more countries do not use hydropower is the high cost. Building new dams is very costly. Some of the dams that already exist are very old. They need to be repaired or replaced. This also costs a lot of money. And building big dams disturbs the habitats of fish and other wildlife. Also, most of the world's major rivers already have dams on them. For these reasons, it is hard to use hydropower much more than it is already being used.

Experts are looking at other sources of hydropower besides river dams. They are looking at ocean waves. The oceans cover about 70 percent of the earth's surface. Ocean waves are very strong. Wave power is not yet widely used. But its use is beginning to expand.

Hydroelectric Power from Niagara Falls

Niagara Falls is the biggest waterfall in North America. It has been used to make power since 1895. The Sir Adam Beck power plant makes power for Ontario, Canada. It makes one-fourth of the power used in Ontario.

The plant is about 4 miles (6km) below the ground. Water from the falls is sent through two tunnels down to the plant. About 475,500 gallons (1.8 million L) of water per second flow through the tunnels.

In 2005 the plant began to build a third tunnel. It will cost $600 million to build. About 132,086 gallons (500,000L) of water per second will flow through the new tunnel. It will increase the amount of electricity the plant makes by 14 percent. The tunnel is expected to be finished in 2009. It will be 6.4 miles (10.4km) long. The tunnel will be one of the largest ever built in North America.

In September 2007 the United Kingdom started to build the world's first wave farm. It will be finished in 2009. It will have 30 wave-energy devices. These will be on the surface of the sea. The wave farm is about 10 miles (16km) off shore. It will cover an area about 1.25 miles by 2.5 miles (2km by 4km). Many companies will be allowed to "plug into" the wave farm. This is so they can test their wave-energy devices. The wave farm will

Niagara Falls has been making power since 1895.

help companies figure out the best ways to get power from the oceans.

Tidal power is similar to ocean wave power. It uses the rise and fall in a river's or ocean's tides to make power. Tidal power is also not widely used yet. But it may be used more in the future. Some countries that already use tidal power include Canada, China, France, Mexico, and Russia. The largest tidal station in the world is on the Rance River in France. But tidal power only works when the tides are going in or out. That means they only work in the morning and at night.

Both wave power and tidal power are still used on a limited basis. As their use grows, they face problems. They use turbines like windmills, only underwater. So they have many of the same problems with wildlife as windmills. The spinning blades can kill or trap fish. And building wave power stations and tidal power stations can disrupt the habitat of fish and other wildlife as well.

From the earliest sails on boats and waterwheels in rivers, people have been using wind and water to make power for centuries. Today both ways of making power are becoming more and more important as people search for clean, safe energy sources.

Chapter 4

Biofuel and Geothermal Energy

J osh Tickell had a dream. He was just out of college. He drove across the United States in a van. But his van did not use gasoline. Instead it was fueled by used cooking oil. Tickell got the oil from fast-food restaurants.

Tickell named his van "the Veggie Van." He drove nearly 10,000 miles (16,000km). He visited 25 states. Over 40 million people saw the Veggie Van. The windows had the words "Powered by Vegetable Oil" [23] painted on them.

The *Los Angeles Times* reported, "When they stopped for a fill-up, it was not at a service station, but at a McDonald's or Kentucky Fried Chicken." [24]

That was in 1997. Tickell still drives the 3-ton (2.7t) Veggie Van. It can go 70 miles per hour (113km/h). It gets 25 miles per gallon (100km/12L). The Veggie Van is blue with big golden sunflowers painted on its sides. And the exhaust smells like french fries. Tickell has driven over 25,000 miles (40,234km) to teach people about biodiesel. He wants more people to use it as a fuel.

Biodiesel is one kind of biofuel. Biofuel comes from living material on the earth's surface, such as plants. This living material is burned to make energy. Because it can reuse "leftovers" like used cooking oil, it is a form of recycling. This is good for the planet.

Biofuel

Biofuel is made from many different oils. These oils include soybean, corn, and canola. Leftover cooking oil from kitchens and restaurants can be used. Animal fat is also used to make biodiesel fuel. It is usually mixed with regular diesel fuel that comes from fossils.

Biodiesel is better for the air than fossil fuels. Cars and trucks that use it pollute less. It is also renewable. That means it can be replaced. Biodiesel comes from plants and animals. More plants and animals can always be grown.

The biggest biodiesel plant in the United States is in Washington State. It opened in 2007. It can make 100 million gallons (379 million L) of biodiesel a year. That is more than was made in the entire United States in 2005. In 2007, 148 plants existed in the United States. Most of them made less than 10 million gallons (38 million L) a year. The plant in Washington is ten times larger than any other plant in the nation.

Country singer Willie Nelson sells his own brand of biodiesel. He calls it BioWillie. It is made from vegetable oils. One writer says, "The exhaust from Mr. Nelson's diesel-powered Mercedes smells like peanuts, or French fries, or whatever alternative fuel happens to be in his tank." [25]

Nelson explains why he likes using biodiesel in his car: "I get better gas mileage, it runs better, the motor runs cleaner, so I swear by it." [26]

E85 blends gas with grain alcohol distilled from corn.

Another type of biofuel is ethanol. It is made from corn and other plants. Brazil makes ethanol from sugarcane. It is the world leader in ethanol. Thirty percent of the fuel used in Brazilian cars is ethanol. Gasoline there must contain at least 20 percent ethanol. And about half of all cars in Brazil can use pure ethanol as fuel. The ethanol there costs about 30 percent less than gasoline.

There are several reasons biofuel is not used more. The raw materials used are usually sugarcane, corn, or soybeans. These can be very costly. In the

United States the main source of biofuel is corn. Some biodiesel plants have had a hard time finding enough corn. Or the corn costs too much for the plant to keep running. As one expert puts it, "The days of cheap grain are gone."[27]

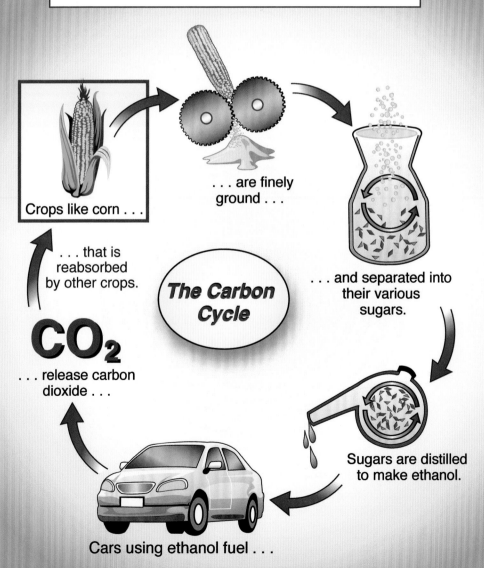

Ethanol: The Cleaner Fuel

Crops like corn . . .

. . . are finely ground . . .

. . . and separated into their various sugars.

The Carbon Cycle

. . . that is reabsorbed by other crops.

CO_2

. . . release carbon dioxide . . .

Sugars are distilled to make ethanol.

Cars using ethanol fuel . . .

The Chicken-Fat Buses of UGA

Forty-seven buses are used at the University of Georgia. All of them use a special blend of fuel. It is made from chicken fat. The bus system is the second largest in the state. About 8 million people ride these buses each year.

The buses use about 300,000 gallons (1 million L) of fuel each year. This fuel costs less than gasoline. It is also cleaner. It pollutes the air less. And the buses smell like chicken when they drive past. This makes the students hungry, especially when it is time for lunch!

Some people worry that all the crops needed to make biofuel could make food cost more. And some people wonder whether it is right to use these crops for something other than food. A man named Gary says, "I find it really disturbing that greed for the almighty dollar is driving farmers to convert FOOD to fuel . . . while each day perhaps as many as 40,000 people die of starvation on this earth!"[28]

Another reason biofuel is not used more is that it can be hard to get it from the plants to the buyers. Ethanol cannot be sent through pipes like regular fuel. That is because it would wear away the pipes. So ethanol must be sent by trains, trucks, and barges instead. These vehicles are all powered by fossil fuels. There are not enough of these in place to keep up with ethanol delivery. It also does not cut down on the use of fossil fuels. And it costs more to send ethanol this way. This adds to the cost of ethanol.

Geothermal

People can also get power from below the earth's surface. This is called geothermal energy. *Geo* means "earth" or "land." *Thermal* means "heat." Geothermal

A drilling rig mines for heat as part of a Swiss geothermal energy project.

energy comes from the intense heat deep inside the earth. Geothermal energy does not pollute.

One country that gets a lot of its power from geothermal energy is Iceland. It is near the Arctic Circle. It is very cold in Iceland. Even in the summer it rarely gets above 60°F (15.5°C). But Iceland has many active volcanoes. Plenty of hot water is generated below the ground. People there use this hot water for heat. They use it directly for space heating. They also use it to make power. Ninety percent of homes there are heated by geothermal power.

Reykjavik is the capital of Iceland. There are lots of hot springs in the area. The water in these hot

Smoky Bay

The year was 874. Ingolfur Arnarson was a Viking from Norway. He was on a long voyage through the cold sea. Finally he sighted land. He threw some wooden posts overboard. Then he waited to see where the posts would wash ashore. That would be where the gods wanted him to settle.

Later Arnarson's slaves found the posts in a strange bay. They saw "smoke" coming up from the earth. They had never seen such a sight in Norway. Arnarson named his settlement Reykjavik, which means "Smoky Bay."

Arnarson was the first person to settle Iceland. But the smoke Arnarson and his slaves saw was not smoke at all. It was steam rising from geothermal springs.

springs is around 150°F (66°C). That is near the surface. Deeper down it is even hotter. One scientist in Iceland put a thermometer down a deep hole. He was looking for a better source of geothermal power. He got a big surprise: "We melted the thermometer," he says. "It was set for 379°C [715°F]; but it just melted. The temperature could have been 399°C [750°F] or even 496°C [925°F]." [29]

Geothermal Energy

Over half the people of Iceland live in or near Reykjavik. The Nesjavellir plant there pumps 14.5 billion gallons (55 billion L) of water a year. That is enough to heat 35,000 homes for 150,000 people. There are over 2,000 miles (3,219km) of underground pipes in Reykjavik. The pipes move the hot water to places that need the heat. This way of heating does not cost much money. In Reykjavik some streets and sidewalks are even heated in the winter.

Geothermal energy comes from heat that starts at the earth's core. This heat makes its way to the surface in the form of volcanoes, geysers, and hot springs. But this happens only in certain areas. Most geothermal activity happens in the areas that surround the Pacific Ocean. This area is known as the Ring of Fire.

The Geysers Geothermal Field is near Santa Rosa, California. It makes enough power for 2 million people. The city of Santa Rosa also adds 11 million gallons (42 million L) of treated sewage a day to the Geysers Geothermal Field. This helps

the plant make more power. So far the city has recycled 15 billion gallons (57 billion L) of sewage. The mayor of Santa Rosa is Bob Blanchard. He says, "How can we get any more environmentally sustainable than to reuse our treated wastewater to help create electricity?" [30]

The Geysers Geothermal Field is the biggest of its kind in the world. This is one reason the United States is the world leader in geothermal power. The United States makes about 36 percent of the world's geothermal power. The Philippines ranks second after the United States. It makes about 23 percent of the world's geothermal power. Four Philippine islands have geothermal power plants. These plants make 27 percent of the country's power.

Geothermal energy is a safe and clean way to get power. But there is one main reason it is not used more. People have to be close to the source of the heat to be able to use it. The hot water or steam loses its heat if it is sent far away. Drilling into the earth to get to the hot water can also make the ground unstable. This may lead to an increase in earthquakes and volcanoes.

There is no one perfect source of energy. Every source has its own problems. A source may be very costly. It may work only when the sun shines. It may work only in certain areas of the world. It may make radioactive waste that has to be safely discarded. Or it may damage land with large dams, wind farms, or sun farms. The best alternative may be to use different sources at different times.

It is also important to conserve energy. This means not using more power than is needed. Because using less power means having to make less power. That may be the most important solution of all.

Notes

Introduction: Alternative Energy at Work

1. David Shukman, "Power Station Harnesses Sun's Rays," BBC News, May 2, 2007. http://news.bbc.co.uk/2/hi/science/nature/6616651.stm.

Chapter 1: Solar Energy

2. Quoted in Tyler Hamilton, "Ontario Goes Solar," TheStar.com, April 26, 2007. www.thestar.com/Business/article/207415.
3. Quoted in Jennifer Kwan, "Ontario Gets Solar Farm," Topix, April 27, 2007. www.topix.net/content/reuters/1007063702201555978533768315540970145360.
4. Quoted in EcoKids Blog, "Our Planet, Our Future," May 1, 2007. http://ecokids.ca/blog/?p=51.
5. American Energy Independence, "America's Solar Energy Potential." www.americanenergyindependence.com/solarenergy.html.
6. Treehugger, April 6, 2007. www.treehugger.com/files/2007/04/solar_power_world.php.

7. Samantha Dlomo, "The Learning Revolution," Solar Electric Light Fund: Solar Schools, Brighter Future. www.self.org/SamanthaDlomo.asp.

8. Quoted in New Jersey Institute of Technology, "New Flexible Plastic Solar Panels Are Inexpensive and Easy to Make," *Science Daily*, July 19, 2007. www.sciencedaily.com/releases/2007/07/070719011151.htm.

Chapter 2: Nuclear Energy and Hydrogen

9. Quoted in Mary Ann Albright, "Expert: Reuse Nuclear Waste," *Gazette-Times*, January 31, 2006. www.gazettetimes.com/articles/2006/02/01/news/community/wedloc02.txt.

10. Quoted in Steve Kroft, "France: Vive les Nukes," CBS News.com, April 8, 2007. www.cbsnews.com/stories/2007/04/06/60minutes/main2655782.shtml.

11. Quoted in Sarah Schafer, "China Leaps Forward," *Newsweek*, February 6, 2006. www.msnbc.msn.com/id/11080908/site/newsweek.

12. Quoted in RP News Wires, "Hydrogen Fuel Cell Vehicle Sets Land Speed Record," Reliable Plant. www.reliableplant.com/article.asp?articleid=7866.

13. Quoted in Elisabeth Bumiller, "Energy Politics on Earth Day as Bush Tours California," *New York Times*, April 23, 2006. http://select.ny

times.com/gst/abstract.html?res=F30611F63E5B
0C708EDDAD0894DE404482&showabstr
act=1.

14. Honda, "The Honda FCX." http://corporate.
honda.com/environment/fuel_cells.aspx?id=fuel
_cells_fcx.

15. Tara Weingarten, "Road Test: Honda FCX
Concept," *Newsweek*, December 18, 2006.
www.msnbc.msn.com/id/16127379/site/news
week.

Chapter 3: Energy from Wind and Water

16. Agence France Presse, "Offshore Wind Farm
Opens off the Coast of the Netherlands,"
International Herald Tribune, April 18, 2007.
www.iht.com/articles/2007/04/18/business/
wind.php.

17. Shell, "The Netherlands' Cleanest Power Plant
Off to a Good Start," April 18, 2007. www.shell.
com/home/content/media-en/news_and_
library/press_releases/2007/winfdarm_egmond_in
auguration_18042007.html.

18. Elizabeth Blunt, "Exploiting Wind Power in
Holland," BBC News, November 13, 2000.
http://news.bbc.co.uk/1/hi/world/europe/1021
714.stm.

19. Associated Press, "European Wind Power Companies Grow in U.S.," MSNBC.com, April 25,
2007. www.msnbc.msn.com/id/18310987.

20. Jiminy Peak Mountain Resort, "Wind Turbine FAQ's." http://green.jiminypeak.com/page.php?PageID=302.
21. Associated Press, "European Wind Power Companies Grow in U.S."
22. Bruce Kennedy, "China's Three Gorges Dam," CNN.com. www.cnn.com/SPECIALS/1999/china.50/asian.superpower/three.gorges.

Chapter 4: Biofuel and Geothermal Energy

23. Josh and Kiara Tickell, "On the Smell of an Oily French Fry," Experiments in Non-Conventional Energy Technologies. www.linux-host.org/energy/sdiesel.html.
24. Quoted in the Veggie Van Organization, "Biodiesel Education." www.veggievan.org.
25. Danny Hakim, "His Car Smelling Like French Fries, Willie Nelson Sells Biodiesel," *New York Times*, December 30, 2005. www.nytimes.com/2005/12/30/business/30biowillie.html?ei=5088&en=3b0ae71846ac300a&ex=1293598800&adxnnl=1&partner=rssnyt&emc=rss&adxnlx=1188831939-TbDpU+CpmcW33fdT6bkVIQ.
26. Quoted in Hakim, "His Car Smelling Like French Fries, Willie Nelson Sells Biodiesel."
27. Quoted in Scott Kilman, "Grocery Bills to Soar as Grain Prices Surge," *Wall Street Journal*, September 28, 2007. http://money.aol.com/

news/articles/_a/grocery-bills-to-soar-as-grain-prices/20070928071909990001?ncid=NWS0 0010000000001.

28. Quoted in AutoblogGreen, "Chevy Describes Its Car as 'Vegetarian' in TV Ad," October 8, 2007. www.autobloggreen.com/2007/10/08/ chevy-describes-its-car-as-vegetarian-in-tv-ad.

29. Quoted in Martin Redfern, "Drilling into a Hot Volcano," BBC News, March 26, 2006. http:// news.bbc.co.uk/2/hi/science/nature/48465 74.stm.

30. Quoted in Calpine, "Investor Relations: News Releases." http://phx.corporate-ir.net/phoenix. zhtml?c=103361&p=irol-newsArticle&ID= 1040696.

Glossary

biodiesel: A type of biofuel.

biofuel: Fuel that is made from living material such as plants or animal waste.

element: A basic substance that cannot be broken down into a smaller substance through an ordinary chemical reaction.

geothermal energy: Geothermal energy comes from the intense heat deep inside the earth.

global warming: A gradual rise in the earth's temperature. It is caused by too much carbon dioxide and other gases that trap the sun's heat in the earth's atmosphere.

greenhouse gases: Gases such as carbon dioxide and methane in the earth's atmosphere that help hold in heat.

hydroelectric: Something that makes electricity using the movement of water.

hydropower: Electricity that is made using waterpower.

nuclear reactor: A large machine that makes nuclear energy by splitting atoms.

radioactive: Something that gives off harmful, poisonous rays.

renewed: Replaced.

solar panel: A panel that gathers sunlight and changes it into electricity.

solar power: Power that comes from the sun.

turbine: Any device that makes power by using the movement of steam, air, or water to turn the blades of a wheel. A windmill that is used to make electricity is called a turbine.

Bibliography

Books

Julie Kerr Casper, *Energy.* New York: Chelsea House, 2007. This book examines various forms of alternative energy, including water, wind, solar, and biofuels, in a format that is easy to follow.

Allison Stark Draper, *Hydropower of the Future: New Ways of Turning Water into Energy.* New York: Rosen, 2003. This book explains hydropower in simple language.

John Giacobello, *Nuclear Power of the Future: New Ways of Turning Atoms into Energy.* New York: Rosen, 2003. With lots of color pictures and text that is easy to follow, this book explains how nuclear power works.

Chris Hayhurst, *Hydrogen Power of the Future: New Ways of Turning Fuel Cells into Energy.* New York: Rosen, 2003. This book uses kid-friendly language to explain the concept of hydrogen fuel cells.

Richard Spilsbury and Louise Spilsbury, *The Earth's Resources.* New York: Chelsea House, 2006. The importance of biomass, hydropower, solar power, and geothermal power as alternative forms of energy are discussed.

Web Sites

Energy Kid's Page (www.eia.doe.gov/kids/energy facts/index.html). This kid-friendly Web site explains the facts about a variety of energy sources, including renewable and nonrenewable sources.

Energy Quest (www.energyquest.ca.gov/story/index.html). This Web site's "Energy Story" contains a table of contents with links to twenty chapters about energy.

How Stuff Works (www.howstuffworks.com). This Web site explains everything you need to know about alternative energy in easy-to-understand language.

Kids Saving Energy (www1.eere.energy.gov/kids/index.html). This Web site for kids contains a wealth of current information on all forms of alternative energy.

Index

Picture Credits

Cover photo: © Construction Photography/Corbis
Maury Aaseng, 11, 27, 45
AP images, 8, 22
AP Images/Sandro Campardo, 25
AP Images/Damian Dovarganes, 36
AP Images/Du Huaju, 35
AP Images/Jackie Johnston, 10
AP Images/Chris Kasson, 44
AP Images/Georgios Kefalas, 47
AP images/Charlie Neibergall, 43
AP Images/Mike Penprase, 17
AP Images/Heribert Proepper, 30, 31 (inset)
AP Images/Eric Risberg, 50
AP Images/Bill Zimmer, 15
ComstockImages/JupiterImages Unlimited, 5, 31 (left)
Goodshoot/JupiterImages Unlimited, 39
Photos.com/JupiterImages Unlimited, 13, 20, 38

About the Author

Cherese Cartlidge holds a bachelor's degree in psychology and a master's degree in middle school education. She has taught reading, language arts, and math. She currently works as a freelance writer and editor and has written seven books for children and young adults.